CLEARING

THE AIR

To all people who are tired
of feeling bogged down
by constrictions and restrictions
but who seek and give
motivation to break free
by speaking up and reaching out

CLEARING THE AIR

Written By
Mylia Tiye Mal Jaza

Feature Image By
Godisable Jacob

Cover Design By
Sun Child Wind Spirit

Proofread By
Dr. Mari Michelle

Clearing The Air

Author
Mylia Tiye Mal Jaza
GoddessSage@bepublished.biz
www.myliajaza.gqnu.net

Self-Publishing Associate
BePublished.Org - Chicago
Dr. Mary M. Jefferson
70 W. Madison, #1400 - Chicago, IL 60602
(972) 880-8316
www.bepublished.org

First Edition.
Printed In the USA. Recycled Paper Encouraged.

TABLE OF CONTENTS

Chapter One

There is one thing that you nor I can do. Despite all our achievements and our current positioning to see our latest accomplishments cash in, we all know we're not doing this one thing that we sometimes trick ourselves into believing we are. And that is, accepting that while we may not be right about every single person, situation or thing, there are plenty of times when we are right about them each and we should quit doubting ourselves and our intuition (spiritual knowledge).

Yes, each of our life experiences allow us a certain level of increased knowledge. All be it, unless we apply the lesson, it cannot be considered wisdom possessed. Thus, there is no measurable growth -- unless we actually apply each lesson learned and gain the wisdom we should.

This is a daily requirement for the rest of our lives. None of us should ever become complacent with (or nonchalant about) anything. That is, unless it's something we don't really care about.

When your back is against the wall, you either relax or rebound. I am one who will rebound. There is no comfort that I can find with my back against the wall. Being backed into a corner is even worse. That means that I will come out fighting even harder.

Some people are blessed to be favored. I have never been favored by anyone, so I have always known that it was up to me to bless me. I am one of those people who, like a few others, have been mistreated my whole life and dealt one unnecessary heap of mess after another. Life taught me early that it's not wise for me to expect to receive the good I give.

Inexperienced and religious people who are new to their spiritual walk come up with all kinds of ignorant and superficial clichés to say to deny or excuse this reality when people mention it. Well, really, not just this but anything. How many times have you been told these same things when you were dealing with something tragic or difficult – and the words came across as empty as they actually were?

"Just pray about it and it will be okay."

"You always think you're being singled out."

"That's not what I meant to say, you misunderstood."

"If you take one step, God will take two."

I'M GOING TO OVERLOOK ALL THAT KIND OF TALK FROM NOW ON! I encourage you and everyone I love to do the same. Any pain we've endured belongs only to that moment in which it occurred. Why prolong your own suffering by not dealing with a situation right then?

"Nip it in the bud," is actually one of the few clichés that have value. Apply it as soon as possible because, as you know, more trouble is always en route. So, the sooner you deal with and heal from the current one, the more moments you'll have in happiness instead of in a hot mess.

I take comfort knowing that every single solitary thing that we are told is supposed to be done in order to get a certain thing are the things I have always done only to see that there's obviously a new set of rules in place exclusively for me.

If you happen to feel the same way because your life has taught you those same undesirable lessons, I regret that. I don't want anyone to have a life that's as cruel as mine. Whatever additional tears you feel the need to shed, let them flow. Whatever hurt you feel, let it go. Then, look forward to never carrying around the burden of such unpleasant experiences as you free your mind from those unworthy memories.

Let me give you some examples by going ahead and cleaning my own dome about specific dirty laundry I find embarrassing. This quick clearing of the air over the African Diaspora is just the beginning. You'll see. No matter what examples I type here for you to read, you can still think of the same number of other examples of some of the same things.

Sometimes, a group of people can be deprived of something for so long that when they do access it they cannot even accept they are receiving or have possession of it because they wanted it to be more substantial. We see this all the time.

Some people even are aware of the lie perpetuated by many when they call for something they already have. Let me just say it this way, because I don't want there to be any confusion about all the different things I've said with this book. **The most repeated lie you will ever hear is that Black people don't stick together.** That is a blatant lie. It is a divisive lie. It is a disgusting lie. Yet, a number of copper-hued people from all over the world (especially those in

America) repeat this malicious prevarication continually and publicly.

One day on an ARTiculation Radio Show episode (articulationmedia.club), I began a social media campaign to debunk myths (#StopTheLies). The campaign was officially started in 2018 when I first began making posts on social media addressing various examples of known lies that need to stop being spread.

This month, I asked other people to mention myths they want busted. To find that out of almost 5,000 people, fewer than 10 wanted to expose a lie. Of course, the assumed reasons for others opting to remain silent were displayed when a couple of people posted comments attacking some of the Truth Speakers.

Let me share the comments with you so you can judge whether any of these would offend you. Also, contemplate whether and what you would have responded. But first, for perspective's sake, I'll tell you the question asked in my post: **"What popular myth do you hear often and you want people to stop spreading the lie?"**

"That Jesus is God."

"Black men are deadbeat fathers."

"The New Testament comes to mind."

"Big men can't fuck and only think bout food."

"The savior story, the light of the world story, Jesus story."

"Men don't practice chivalry maybe not da ones yall choose to date but."

"Small people big appetite."

"That light skin women feel they are better than dark skin women! I hate hearing it! We are the same."

"That all Black people are Israelites when the scriptures plainly state that spiritual Israel

are only the prophets alone, making them *The Promise Seed* and *Seed of Promise*. *These Hebrews suffer from Babylonia=Confusion of Tongues.*"

"*Mylia, I guess I'm beginning to see how everyone is on their own journey, and how they view the world is unique to their perspective.. Myth to me can be truth to someone else. I'm just responsible for my own reality and how I navigate through this life path . . . We have to learn to understand how to use the energies around us. Allowing people to be happy, it's more important than me being right.*"

"*Black people don't stick together or help each other like other races.*"

So, would you have posted a public response to expose a myth, express your desire to not entertain the topic, or fought someone else's effort to express the truth? I won't even bother to jot down the zealous, jealous and expected negativity that was posted. You can't ignore all bad things, but you can ignore some (as even the comments shared display). Reality is, some people have reprobated minds and they not only love lies, they love the way they sound lying, and they will do anything to silence truth.

More often than not, our staying quiet and "lowly" won't ever vindicate us. Some other event will need to happen in order for us to have another shot at that. At the end of the day, just like everything else they avoid "action" for whatever reason, we're just delaying doing what needs to be done because they think things will get better on its own.

We know this and everyone needs to admit it. What's the point of continuing to procrastinate on speaking up for yourself – or truth? Who's approval or favor are you hoping to FINALLY receive?

It should be your own preference you seek, since you are the only one with you 24 hours a day all seven days of the week. Now is the time for us to clean house, air dirty laundry, and clear the air!

How else can you truly expect to live a healthy life wholly? We all know that filthy places are not healthy, and are not safe for prolonged occupation. Protect yourself to assure you don't catch any *dis-ease*.

As this new year begins, clean your slate and be bold embarking on your realized path of "truth despite brutality." Be fearless and frank. Be candid and courageous. Be any good thing other than the person who keeps allowing themselves to be misled, mistreated, silenced, and left feeling defeated.

Get your power back by removing everything blocking it – starting with you.

That reminds me of a few more clichés. These are some of the good ones that you do need to heed.

"Get out of your own way."

"There's nothing to fear but fear itself."

"If you don't take care of you, you can't take care of anybody else."

People ask why trauma survivors take years to tell their stories, and we all know they all know why the victims of these crimes do so. The same goes for when people immediately speak up. That's whey you hear people say things like, "It was a setup. How they get all that information that quick." People who are approval seekers do and say all kinds of senseless things.

You are one who has no reason to seek approval. After all, as I've said in other works after confessing to others aloud for years, I require no outside validation and my freedom to express is endless – limited only by the constraints my own health dictates. I hope you feel the same about your life too.

Stress remains the top killer. Stress feeds into so much we do in life, even when we try to push it back and especially when we focus on it. I am the type of personality for whom remaining silent or bound in stressful situations is an absolute no-no. I immediately speak up, and I crank it up if the offensive actions / words don't cease. This habit may be the reason why, despite my having survived more strokes than anyone I personally know or have heard of (and to be pretty much 95% myself), no one can tell by talking to me or being around me in personal and business milieus.

But, as my book <u>When The Quarterback Got Cut</u> revealed about seven years ago, I too held a "secret" from the world for 20 years. I've held more secrets for longer than that, and so have you and everyone else. None of us should continue allowing people to attack any Truth Speakers under any circumstances and in any form.

Because really, when rape and molestation sufferers and survivors (or anyone else not lying) speak out, whether the opposition likes what is revealed or not, it's only right to respond the way you would want to be treated when you were the one confessing. After all, which side are you on? You only have two choices no matter how you break it down. Morality is a law of the heart.

What's written on yours?
Where does your heart lie?

THE ART & ARTIST

Sometimes, we have to clean house, air dirty laundry, and clear the air. As this new year begins, clean your slate and be bold embarking on your realized path. Be fearless and frank. Be candid and courageous. Be any good thing other than the person who keeps 

allowing themselves to be misled, mistreated, silenced, and left feeling defeated. Get your power back by removing everything blocking it – starting with you.

Published with assistance from BePublished.org in January 2019, **<u>CLEARING THE AIR</u>** by Mylia Tiye Mal Jaza is the author's 28th published work and her first of 12 solely dedicated to utilizing "fear-facing" or "embarrassment therapy" to push herself and others away from any lingering fears that keep them trapped by lies and prevent them from completing goals or finding prolonged peace.

Available for order worldwide as a Kindle ebook for $9.95 (plus tax), **<u>CLEARING THE AIR</u>** is also available as a softcover book for $14.95 (plus tax/shipping) from bricks-and-mortar and online book retailers including Barnes & Noble, your local bookstore, and Amazon.Com.

THE ARTIST

Mylia Tiye Mal Jaza (Mary "Mari" Michelle Jefferson) is a former Texas resident and Mississippi native presently residing in Illinois. The author of 25 works to date, the 44-year-old vows to continue publishing at least one book each year for the rest of her life.

Mylia is a graduate of Jackson State University and the University of Texas at Dallas. She also holds an honorary doctorate degree from Trinity Evangelical

Christian University. In Summer 2017, she was awarded two certificates from Harvard University for successfully completing courses weeks early with high marks.

The entrepreneur, former professional model, and wedding officiant is also an award-winning journalist who gives back to the communities in which she lives and conducts business by mentoring teens, cleaning highways, feeding the homeless, helping build houses, providing gifts to nursing home residents, organizing community art exhibits and music festivals, and conducting school supplies drives for youth.

Also known as the visual artist Sun Child Wind Spirit, Jaza (aka Goddess Sage) is a well-known vocalist who has performed alongside international artists and at popular venues. She also helps writers with an array of editorial and business services including self-publishing and promotions training through BePublished.Org.

Prior to starting **CLEARING THE AIR** in January 2019 and releasing it the following week, three of Mylia's published books were works she published that were written by relatives/ancestors of hers – <u>The Facts Of Reconstruction *by John R. Lynch*</u>, <u>The Old Negro And The New Negro *by T. Leroy Jefferson, M.D.*</u>, and <u>Mother's Mantras *by Susie W. Jefferson*</u>.

Mylia's other books were original works she created that ranged in content from poetry and prose to film and television scripts. The titles include: <u>Life Is Beautiful: La Vita E Bella</u>, <u>Seen In Other Words</u>, <u>Plea For Peace</u>, <u>All For Show</u>, <u>Scientific Evidence God Exists</u>, <u>Elegies Of A Goddess</u>, <u>When The Quarterback Got Cut</u>, <u>Get Off Your Packages</u>, <u>Stop & Tie Your Shoes</u>, <u>Amour Noir</u>, <u>The Blessed Blessing</u>,

Breaking Every Curse, _Tainted Fruit_ and
The Middle Child.

MarryUsNow.us
PeopleWarmer.com

www.ingramcontent.com/pod-product-compliance
Lightning Source LLC
Chambersburg PA
CBHW051426250726
48655CB00003B/1253